Leveled by an EARTHQUAKE!

by Adam Reingold

Consultant: Keith C. Heidorn, Ph.D.
CMOS Accredited Consulting Meteorologist (retired)
Publisher and Editor of *The Weather Doctor* Web site

BEARPORT
PUBLISHING

New York, New York

Credits

Cover, © Bagus Indahono/epa/Corbis and © Ryan Pyle/Corbis; Title Page, © Ryan Pyle/Corbis; TOC, © Dariusz Kantorski/Shutterstock; 4, © Guangzhou Integrated Image Co., Ltd./fotoe; 5, © AP Images/Andy Wong; 7, © AP Images/Andy Wong; 8L, © Xinhua/Landov; 8R, © Agence France-Presse/AFP/Getty Images; 9, © Natalie Behring/ Aurora Photos; 10L, © Xinhua/Landov; 10R, © Imaginechina via AP Images; 11T, © Xinhua/Landov; 11B, © Xinhua/ Landov; 14, © AP Images/Nicky Loh; 15, © Xinhua/Landov; 16, © James Benet/iStockphoto; 17, © Science & Society Picture Library/Getty Images; 18, © Tom Bean/Corbis; 20, © Otto Greule Jr./Getty Images; 21T, © Lloyd Cluff/Corbis; 21B, © Roger Ressmeyer/Corbis; 22T, ©Philip Gordon/Imagestate Media Partners Limited-Impact Photos/Alamy; 22B, Courtesy of Earthquake Country Alliance/Southern California Earthquake Center at USC; 23, © AP Images/ Oded Balilty; 24, Courtesy of The National Science Foundation; 25T, © Peter Essick/Aurora Photos; 25B, © Nagaoka University of Technology/Project I Ltd.; 26, © AP Images/Andy Wong; 27, © AP Images/Andy Wong; 28, © AP Images/ Dita Alangkara; 29, © Supri/Reuters/Landov.

Publisher: Kenn Goin
Senior Editor: Lisa Wiseman
Creative Director: Spencer Brinker
Design: Dawn Beard Creative
Photo Researcher: Omni-Photo Communications, Inc.

Library of Congress Cataloging-in-Publication Data

Reingold, Adam.
  Leveled by an earthquake! / by Adam Reingold.
    p. cm. — (Disaster survivors)
  Includes bibliographical references and index.
  ISBN-13: 978-1-936087-53-2 (lib. bdg.)
  ISBN-10: 1-936087-53-7 (lib. bdg.)
  1. Earthquakes—Juvenile literature. 2. Emergency management—Juvenile literature.
  I. Title.
  QE521.3.R45 2010
  551.22—dc22
                                2009036961

For more information, write to Bearport Publishing Company, Inc., 101 Fifth Avenue, Suite 6R, New York, New York 10003. Printed in the United States of America in North Mankato, Minnesota.

122009
090309CGD

10 9 8 7 6 5 4 3 2 1

Contents

Earthquake!

It was 2:27 P.M. on May 12, 2008, in Beichuan (BAY-chwan), China. Sixteen-year-old Li Anning and her classmates were in the middle of a geography lesson. From her classroom on the fourth floor of her school, Anning could see the nearby mountains. Classes would soon be over for the day. Anning would then be able to hang out with her friends.

This building was one of several that made up Li Anning's school, Beichuan Middle School.

A minute later, at 2:28 P.M., the lives of Anning and millions of others changed forever. "Our classroom began to shake," she said. "In no time, the fifth, fourth, and third floors collapsed." What had happened? The Great Sichuan (SIH-chwan) **Earthquake** had just struck.

Anning's school was buried under a pile of huge rocks and dirt. Only a basketball hoop (lower left) was left standing.

basketball hoop

At least 69,000 people were

A School Disappears

Seconds later, Anning felt the ground shake from several more **tremors**. When the nearby mountains shook, a huge amount of loose earth began to slide toward the school. Within seconds, the building was buried completely. Anning and her schoolmates were trapped under the great weight of cracked concrete floors and broken walls. Some could not move. Others could barely breathe. "We have to keep going so we can get through this," said one classmate.

Where the Great Sichuan Earthquake Occurred

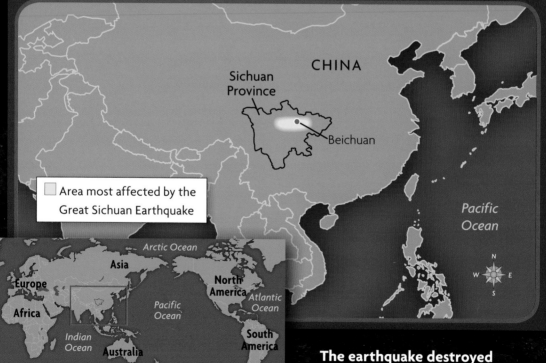

CHINA

Sichuan Province

Beichuan

☐ Area most affected by the Great Sichuan Earthquake

Pacific Ocean

Arctic Ocean

Asia

Europe

North America

Atlantic Ocean

Africa

Pacific Ocean

Indian Ocean

Australia

South America

Southern Ocean

Antarctica

The earthquake destroyed millions of homes and buildings throughout Sichuan Province, located in southern China.

For hours Anning and other **survivors** waited for help. To make themselves feel better, they sang their favorite songs. Many thought of their families and friends. They hoped that they, too, were alive.

Most of Beichuan was completely destroyed within minutes.

Most deaths from earthquakes occur when people get tr...

Help Has Arrived!

For almost two more days, Anning struggled to live beneath the **rubble**. With every breath she took, she felt pains deep in her body. As each hour passed, she heard fewer sounds from the other students around her. Always though, she heard the voices of parents who had rushed to the school after the earthquake. "Hold on! Help has arrived!" one parent shouted over and over.

A student from Anning's school being rescued

The Great Sichuan Earthquake damaged parts of the Wolong National Nature Reserve in China, where giant pandas live. Most of the animals survived. However, one died and two were hurt. The animals that survived were quickly moved to safer areas.

Panda bears being fed a day after the earthquake

Finally, Anning heard the sounds of workers and cranes. Slowly they removed the heavy rubble that was once her school. Soon she saw the hands of her rescuers. Anning was finally safe!

Rescue workers search for survivors at Anning's school.

Lucky to Be Alive

Earthquakes kill and injure more people each year than most other **natural disasters**. At Anning's school, she and 360 other students and teachers survived. Sadly, many others from her school died.

Most earthquakes are minor and cause little damage or death. Major earthquakes, however, can cause great **devastation**. Not only do they injure and kill people, but they also **level** buildings and can destroy whole towns.

This survivor was trapped for almost eight days beneath a collapsed power station near Beichuan.

After the Great Sichuan Earthquake, many

In Beichuan, most buildings were completely flattened. Streets were split open, many gas lines were broken, and water and sewer pipes were shattered. There was no water, gas, phones, or Internet service for months. It was almost impossible for the people of Beichuan to communicate with the outside world.

After the earthquake, clean water was pumped from fire trucks.

Earthquakes can occur both on land and at sea. Some underwater earthquakes cause giant destructive waves called tsunamis.

Thousands of families had to live in tents for many months after their homes were destroyed.

Earth's Layers

For centuries, people tried to figure out the mystery behind why earthquakes occur. Some believed that earthquakes were **thunderstorms** coming from the belly of Earth. Today, scientists know this is not true. They have learned that Earth is made up of four major layers. The **crust** is the outermost layer and lies on top of the **mantle**, which is the largest layer. Below the mantle is a liquid layer called the outer core. The last layer, located at the center of Earth, is the inner core.

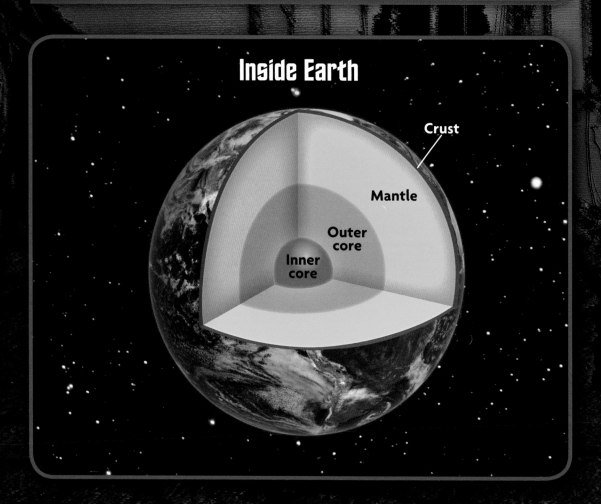

Inside Earth

Crust

Mantle

Outer core

Inner core

From studying these layers, scientists now know that most earthquakes are caused by movements of massive slabs of rock called **tectonic plates**. These plates float on hot, soft parts of Earth's mantle. They move slowly, like icebergs drifting in the oceans.

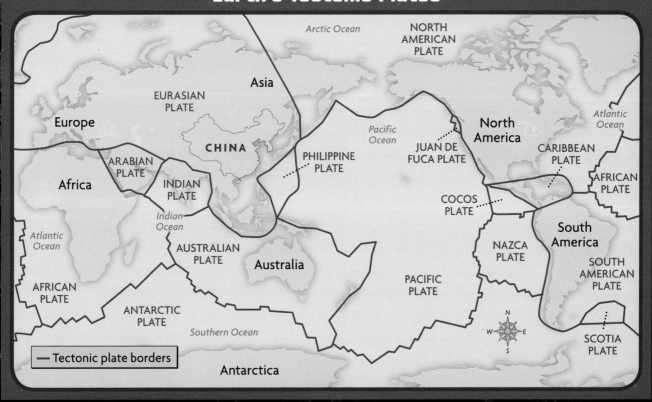

Earth's Tectonic Plates

Arctic Ocean

NORTH AMERICAN PLATE

Asia

EURASIAN PLATE

Europe

Atlantic Ocean

CHINA

Pacific Ocean

North America

JUAN DE FUCA PLATE

CARIBBEAN PLATE

ARABIAN PLATE

PHILIPPINE PLATE

Africa

INDIAN PLATE

AFRICAN PLATE

COCOS PLATE

Indian Ocean

South America

Atlantic Ocean

AUSTRALIAN PLATE

Australia

NAZCA PLATE

AFRICAN PLATE

PACIFIC PLATE

SOUTH AMERICAN PLATE

ANTARCTIC PLATE

Southern Ocean

N
W   E
S

SCOTIA PLATE

— Tectonic plate borders

Antarctica

Scientists have given each tectonic plate a name. China sits on the Eurasian Plate.

Generally, tectonic plates move at the same speed as a person's fingernails grow. That's about 1.4 inches (3.6 cm) every year.

What's Shaking?

Earthquakes can occur when tectonic plates grind against or crash into each other as they move. If one of the plates slips as it pushes against the other, the pressure that has been building up causes huge amounts of energy to be released in the form of **shock waves**. These powerful waves shake Earth's surface as they travel away from the earthquake's epicenter—the area on Earth's surface directly above where the earthquake starts.

How an Earthquake Can Occur

shock waves shaking Earth's surface

plate moving

where the earthquake starts

The epicenter of the Great Sichuan Earthquake was located in the town of Wenchuan (WUHN-chwan), about 96 miles (154 km) from Anning's school. Many buildings in Wenchuan, as shown here, were destroyed.

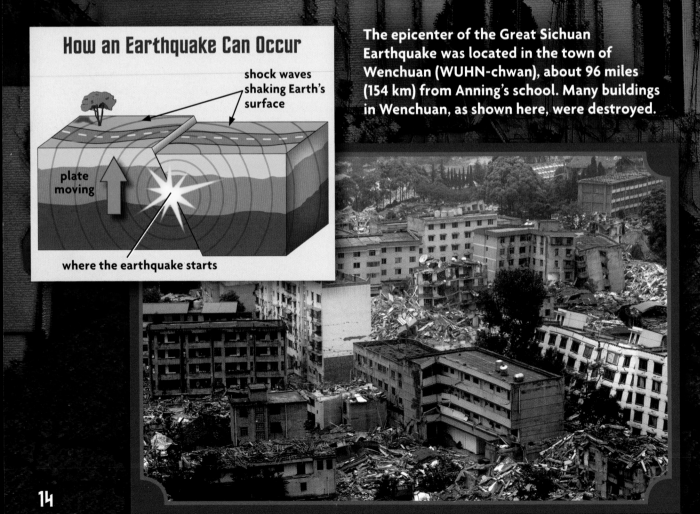

The first shock waves of the Great Sichuan Earthquake raced through Sichuan Province at about 6,935 miles per hour (11,161 kph). The waves quickly crumbled many towns and villages. About fifteen minutes later, a smaller earthquake, called an **aftershock**, hit. It destroyed more buildings and homes. For two weeks following the earthquake, more than 8,000 aftershocks were reported. Almost a year later, aftershocks were still occurring.

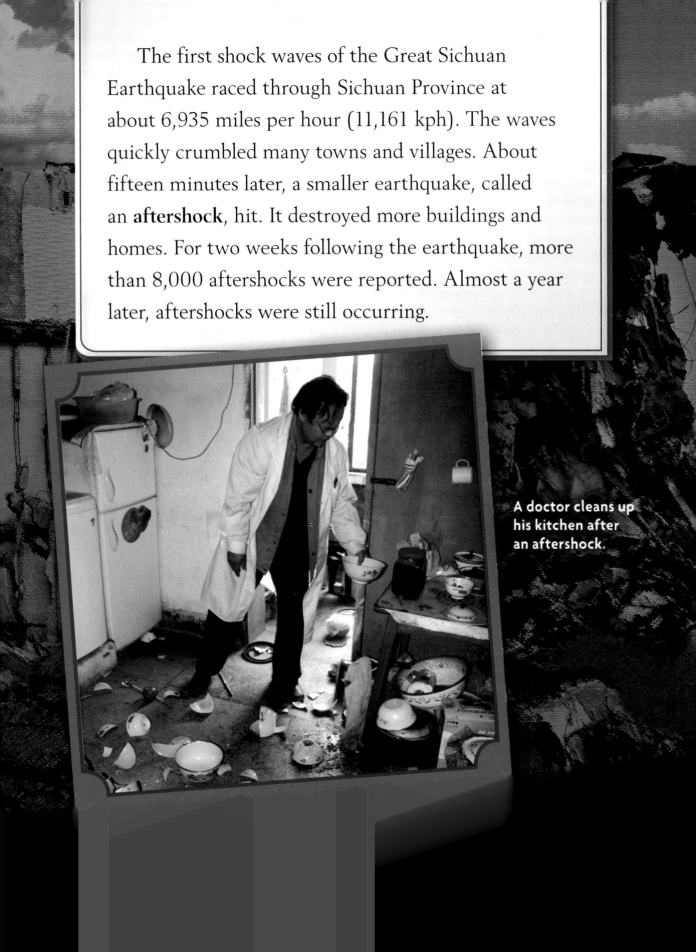

A doctor cleans up his kitchen after an aftershock.

Measuring Earthquakes

Every year thousands of shock waves from earthquakes travel through Earth's surface. Earthquake scientists, called seismologists, have invented a way to measure their size and strength. They use special devices called **seismographs**.

Seismographs such as this one are used to measure earthquakes. Movements of the ground show up as wiggly lines. Short wiggly lines that don't show many wiggles indicate a small earthquake. Longer wiggly lines with many large wiggles indicate a large earthquake.

Once a seismograph records the movement of the ground during a quake, seismologists give the earthquake a number on the **Richter scale** to describe its **magnitude**. A number of 7.0 or above means that the quake was very powerful—such earthquakes last longer and strike a wider area than weaker ones. The Great Sichuan Earthquake measured a magnitude of 8.0 on the Richter scale.

This instrument was used by people in China almost 2,000 years ago to indicate earthquakes. Shock waves would shake the ball out of the mouth of the dragon that was facing the direction of the earthquake. It would then fall into the mouth of the frog. This let people know that an earthquake had occurred.

Scientists also use the moment magnitude scale to measure earthquakes. It measures stronger earthquakes, over 7.0, more accurately than the Richter scale.

The Next "Big One"

Can scientists **predict** earthquakes to help save lives? Unfortunately, no. Most earthquakes catch people by complete surprise. Even with modern measuring instruments, seismologists agree that earthquakes cannot yet be predicted. No one has been able to say the exact time and place when the next "big one" will hit.

However, many seismologists believe that it is possible to identify areas where earthquakes are more likely to strike. These places are usually weak spots in Earth's crust called **faults**. One such area is in California, where the San Andreas Fault lies. This fault stretches across a long part of the state, with areas located close to the large cities of San Francisco and Los Angeles.

Thousands of small earthquakes occur along the San Andreas Fault every year.

One powerful earthquake that struck along the San Andreas Fault occurred in 1906 in San Francisco. The earthquake is believed to have killed about 3,000 people.

Another common place for earthquakes to occur is along the edge of tectonic plates in the "Ring of Fire." About 90 percent of the world's earthquakes happen in this area in the Pacific Ocean. The largest earthquake recorded here happened in Chile in 1960. It measured a magnitude of 9.5 on the Richter scale.

Ring of Fire

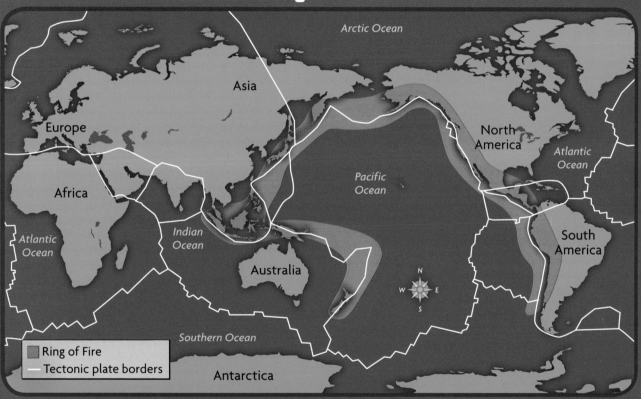

Most of the world's active volcanoes are located along the Ring of Fire. That is how the area got its name.

Anytime, Anyplace

In 1988, scientists indicated that it was "highly probable" that a powerful earthquake would hit near the San Andreas Fault within 30 years. Only a year later, their prediction came true.

On October 17, 1989, an earthquake struck San Francisco. Unlike other quakes, this one was watched by millions of people live on television. It hit just as a World Series baseball game was beginning. Players and fans alike shouted, "Earthquake!" as the field and stadium shook.

Police and emergency workers drove onto the field to help players and fans. Luckily, no one was injured at the stadium.

The World Series Earthquake registered a magnitude of approximately 6.9 on the Richter scale. Sixty-two people were killed, and 3,757 were injured. Many buildings and roads in the area were destroyed.

"I suddenly felt like I was going to fall to the ground," said Billy Bathe, one of the players. "Who would have ever expected a World Series earthquake?"

Houses, bridges, and roadways collapsed during the earthquake. Fires from broken gas pipes burned many buildings.

STOP

21

Inside or Outside?

No matter how big or small, earthquakes can be extremely dangerous. When people feel the ground shaking, they should quickly seek safety.

Experts say it is safest to be outdoors in an open area during an earthquake. It's important for people to stay away from buildings, streetlights, and overhead wires until the shaking stops so that nothing can fall on them.

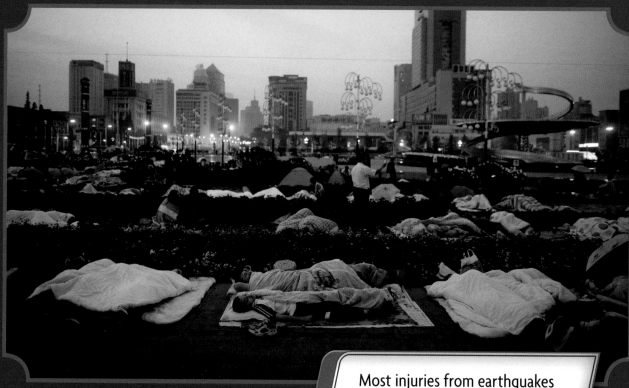

Some survivors from the earthquake in Sichuan Province slept outside to protect themselves from buildings that could collapse from aftershocks.

Most injuries from earthquakes occur when people in a building are hit by falling objects as they try to escape outside while the building is still shaking.

When caught in a house or building during an earthquake, people should quickly look for cover under a sturdy piece of furniture, such as a table, and hold onto it. They should remain there until the shaking stops.

Those who find themselves trapped under a crushed building should call out for help, but not move. They should stay still to avoid kicking up dangerous dust that will make it hard for them to breathe.

In Japan and other countries around the world where earthquakes occur, children take part in earthquake safety drills.

By following these safety tips, people caught in a building during an earthquake can help keep themselves safe.

DROP!   COVER!   HOLD ON!

Learning From Earthquakes

Although earthquakes can happen at anytime and without warning, people can still prepare for them. Scientists believe the best way to protect lives is to build stronger buildings. According to **engineer** Elizabeth Hausler, "Earthquakes don't kill people; bad buildings do."

Engineers built this model building on a special steel base that shakes as if an earthquake is occurring. By studying the effects of the shaking, they can design stonger and safer buildings.

Many engineers believe that it's very difficult to design a building that will remain completely undamaged during powerful earthquakes. Instead, they try to design buildings that can stand up long enough for the people inside to safely escape before the building starts to fall apart.

Engineers spend many hours studying pictures of collapsed buildings from past earthquakes. This helps them come up with new ideas for making buildings safer. One new idea is to use steel bands that "hug" buildings. These bands prevent structures from twisting and falling down during quakes. Another idea is to build special **foundations** that enable buildings to slowly rock back and forth without collapsing during an earthquake.

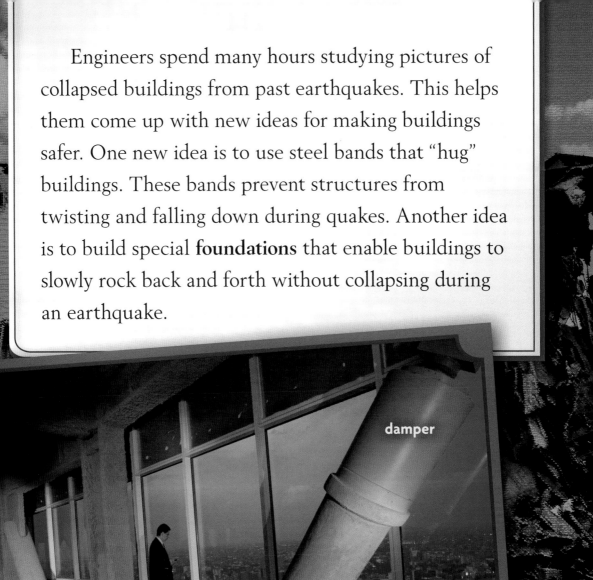

damper

Some buildings are built with parts called dampers that help them stop shaking during an earthquake.

Special vehicles are being designed to carry injured people away from danger during earthquakes.

Survivors Rebuild

What happens to people after surviving a major earthquake? Most rebuild their homes and go on with their lives.

Sometimes, however, the destruction is so great that people can't rebuild. After the Great Sichuan Earthquake, the Chinese government decided to close the city of Beichuan forever and build a memorial park in honor of those who were injured or died. This meant that Anning and her classmates would never again return to their old school.

Beichuan is now closed off forever behind a 12-foot (3.7-m) fence.

Perhaps one day Anning will move to the new city of Beichuan. It is being built 12 miles (19.3 km) away from the old one.

Survivors who live in earthquake areas never forget the power of earthquakes. As they rebuild their lives, they must always be ready for the next "big one."

The new city of Beichuan will be built over the next ten years. It will be smaller than the old Beichuan. When completed, it will have new roads, buildings, houses, and schools to support about 70,000 people.

Planners looking at a site for the new Beichuan

Famous Earthquakes

Throughout history, earthquakes have leveled cities and towns and changed people's lives forever. Here are two of the most powerful earthquakes ever reported.

Prince William Sound, Alaska, 1964

- On March 27 at about 5:36 P.M., a massive earthquake struck Prince William Sound, Alaska. It was estimated to have a magnitude of between 8.6 to 9.2 on the Richter scale.
- The earthquake was the most powerful ever recorded in the United States. It shook for about five minutes, much longer than most powerful earthquakes.
- It created a massive tsunami with waves reported to be more than 220 feet (67 m) high.
- More than 100 people were killed by the earthquake and tsunami.

Villages were completely washed away by the tsunami that hit Indonesia and other countries after a huge underwater earthquake struck.

Sumatra, Indonesia, 2004

- On December 26 at 7:58 A.M., a powerful earthquake struck in the Indian Ocean near the island of Sumatra. It measured a magnitude of about 9.1 on the Richter scale.
- The earthquake created a giant tsunami that traveled as fast as a jet plane, covering about 3,000 miles (4,828 km).
- Huge waves, some up to 100 feet (30 m) high, slammed into cities and villages in South Asia, Southeast Asia, and East Africa.
- About 227,898 people were killed or went missing. Another 1.7 million people were left homeless.

Earthquake Safety

Here are some important earthquake safety tips from the American Red Cross.

☑ If caught indoors, get under a desk or table and stay there. Avoid windows, fireplaces, and very heavy furniture.

☑ Avoid the kitchen in your home, where gas pipes for the oven can burst open and cause a fire. Also, plates and dishes can fall from open cabinets and injure people.

☑ To avoid being hit by falling objects, do not go outside until all shaking stops.

☑ If caught outdoors, find an open area that is far away from power lines and buildings.

☑ If caught in an area near the ocean, always check for tsunami warnings. Head for higher ground when tsunami warnings are issued.

☑ Have a fire extinguisher available for fires that can be caused by earthquakes and other natural disasters.

☑ Have an earthquake survival kit available. It should include the following: a flashlight and radio with extra batteries, enough food and water to last for several days, blankets, and first-aid supplies.

On September 30, 2009, an earthquake measuring about 7.6 on the Richter scale hit Sumatra, Indonesia. It has been estimated that more than 1,000 people were killed.

Glossary

aftershock (AF-tur-shok) a small earthquake that comes after the main earthquake

crust (KRUHST) Earth's hard outer layer

devastation (*dev*-uh-STAY-shuhn) massive destruction caused by an action of people or of nature

earthquake (URTH-kwayk) shaking of the ground caused by the moving of Earth's outer layer

engineer (*en*-juh-NIHR) a person trained to design and build bridges, roads, buildings, or other structures

faults (FAWLTS) large cracks in Earth's crust that can cause earthquakes

foundations (foun-DAY-shuhnz) solid bases on which buildings are built

level (LEV-uhl) to flatten

magnitude (MAG-nuh-tood) the size or intensity of something; scientists describe an earthquake's magnitude using the Richter scale

mantle (MAN-tuhl) the part of Earth between the crust and the outer core

natural disasters (NACH-ur-uhl duh-ZASS-turz) disasters such as earthquakes or tsunamis that are caused by nature rather than by people

predict (pri-DIKT) to tell or describe something before it happens

Richter scale (RIK-tuhr SKAYL) a number system used to indicate the strength of earthquakes; the higher the number, the more powerful the earthquake

rubble (RUHB-uhl) pieces of broken rock, brick, and other building materials

seismographs (SIZE-muh-grafs) machines used for measuring the intensity of earthquakes by recording the seismic waves that they generate

shock waves (SHOK WAYVZ) movements of energy through Earth caused by an earthquake

survivors (sur-VYE-vurz) people who live through disasters or horrible events

tectonic plates (tek-TON-nik PLAYTS) massive slabs of rock that float on Earth's mantle

thunderstorms (THUHN-dur-*stormz*) storms with heavy rain and loud, rumbling sounds that come after a flash of lightning

tremors (TREM-urz) shaking caused by an earthquake

Bibliography

Fradkin, Philip. *Magnitude 8*. New York: Henry Holt (1998).

"Girl Tells How She Went Through Ordeal While Trapped." *China Today* (May 14, 2008). **www.chinatoday.com.cn/English/sichuan/020.htm**

Grace, Catherine O'Neill. *Forces of Nature*. Washington, D.C.: National Geographic Society (2004).

"Survivors: Real Stories About the Earthquake." *Women of China News* (May 22, 2008). **www.womenofchina.cn/news/Spotlight/204038.jsp**

earthquake.usgs.gov/regional/world/historical.php

Read More

Brunelle, Lynn. *Earthquake! The 1906 San Francisco Nightmare.* New York: Bearport (2005).

Butts, Ed. *SOS: Stories of Survival*. Plattsburgh, NY: Tundra (2007).

Fradin, Dennis and Judy. *Witness to Disaster: Earthquakes.* Washington, D.C.: National Geographic Children's Books (2008).

Learn More Online

To learn more about earthquakes, visit
www.bearportpublishing.com/DisasterSurvivors

Index

About the Author

*Adam Reingold is a writer and editor. He also enjoys
walking along the calm waters of the Hudson River in New York City,
where a major earthquake has never been recorded.*